# Demographics and 2008 Run Timing of Adult Lost River (*Deltistes luxatus*) and Shortnose (*Chasmistes brevirostris*) Suckers in Upper Klamath Lake, Oregon, 2008

By Eric C. Janney, Brian S. Hayes, David A. Hewitt, Patrick M. Barry, Alta Scott, Justin Koller, Mark Johnson, and Greta Blackwood

Prepared in cooperation with the Bureau of Reclamation

Open-File Report 2009–1183

U.S. Department of the Interior
U.S. Geological Survey

## U.S. Department of the Interior
KEN SALAZAR, Secretary

## U.S. Geological Survey
Suzette M. Kimball, Acting Director

U.S. Geological Survey, Reston, Virginia: 2009

For more information on the USGS—the Federal source for science about the Earth, its natural and living resources, natural hazards, and the environment, visit *http://www.usgs.gov* or call 1-888-ASK-USGS.

For an overview of USGS information products, including maps, imagery, and publications, visit *http://www.usgs.gov/pubprod*

To order this and other USGS information products, visit *http://store.usgs.gov*

Any use of trade, product, or firm names is for descriptive purposes only and does not imply endorsement by the U.S. Government.

# Contents

# Figures

# Figures—Continued

# Tables

# Conversion Factors and Acronyms

SI to Inch/Pound

| Multiply | By | To obtain |
|----------|-----|-----------|
| Length | | |
| centimeter (cm) | 0.3937 | inch (in.) |
| millimeter (mm) | 0.03937 | inch (in.) |
| meter (m) | 3.281 | foot (ft) |
| kilometer (km) | 0.6214 | mile (mi) |

Temperature in degrees Celsius (°C) may be converted to degrees Fahrenheit (°F) as follows: °F=(1.8×°C)+32.

Temperature in degrees Fahrenheit (°F) may be converted to degrees Celsius (°C) as follows: °C=(°F-32)/1.8.

## Acronyms

| | |
|-----|-----|
| FDX | full-duplex |
| FL | fork length |
| LRS | Lost River sucker |
| PIT | passive integrated transponder |
| SNS | shortnose suckers |
| UKL | Upper Klamath Lake |
| USGS | U.S. Geological Survey |

# Demographics and 2008 Run Timing of Adult Lost River (*Deltistes luxatus*) and Shortnose (*Chasmistes brevirostris*) Suckers in Upper Klamath Lake, Oregon, 2008

By Eric C. Janney, Brian S. Hayes, David A. Hewitt, Patrick M. Barry, Alta Scott, Justin Koller, Mark Johnson, and Greta Blackwood

## Abstract

We used capture–recapture data to assess population dynamics of endangered Lost River suckers (*Deltistes luxatus)* and shortnose suckers (*Chasmistes brevirostris*) in Upper Klamath Lake, Oregon. The Cormack–Jolly–Seber method was used to estimate apparent survival probabilities, and a temporal symmetry model was used to estimate annual seniority probabilities. Information theoretic modeling was used to assess variation in parameter estimates due to time, gender, and species. In addition, length data were used to detect multiple year-class failures and events of high recruitment into adult spawning populations. Survival of adult Lost River and shortnose suckers varied substantially across years. Relatively high annual mortality was observed for the lakeshore-spawning Lost River sucker subpopulation in 2002 and for the river spawning subpopulation in 2001. Shortnose suckers experienced high mortality in 2001 and 2004. This indicates that high mortality events are not only species specific, but also are specific to subpopulations for Lost River suckers. Seniority probability estimates and length composition data indicate that recruitment of new individuals into adult sucker populations has been sparse. The overall fitness of Upper Klamath Lake sucker populations are of concern given the low observed survival in some years and the paucity of recent recruitment. During most years, estimates of survival probabilities were lower than seniority probabilities, indicating net losses in adult sucker population abundances. The evidence for decline was more marked for shortnose suckers than for Lost River suckers. Our data indicated that sucker survival for both species, but especially shortnose suckers, was sometimes low in years without any observed fish kills. This indicates that high mortality can occur over a protracted period, resulting in poor annual survival, but will not necessarily be observed in association with a fish kill. A better understanding of the factors influencing adult survival and recruitment into spawning populations is needed. Monitoring these vital parameters will provide a quantitative means to evaluate population status and assess the effectiveness of conservation and recovery efforts.

# Introduction

Lost River suckers (*Deltistes luxatus*) and shortnose suckers (*Chasmistes brevirostris*) are long-lived, late-maturing catostomids that are endemic to the Upper Klamath River basin in southern Oregon and northern California (Scoppettone and Vinyard, 1991). Historical accounts indicate that both species once were extremely abundant throughout the upper basin and were used in a subsistence fishery by Native Americans and later in a popular recreational snag fishery that was closed in 1987 (Markle and Cooperman, 2002). Declining population abundance trends and range reductions were noted for both species as early as the mid-1960s. The extent of these declines was not evident, however, until the mid-1980s, when recreational catch rates exhibited dramatic decreases that were attributable in part to overfishing (Markle and Cooperman, 2002; National Research Council, 2004). Estimated annual fishery harvest of spawning suckers in the Sprague and Williamson rivers ranged from more than 10,000 fish in 1968 to 687 fish in 1985 (Markle and Cooperman, 2002). In addition to declining catches, age data from suckers collected during a 1986 fish kill indicated that the Lost River sucker (LRS) population was composed of old individuals and that no substantial recruitment had occurred during the previous 15 years (Scoppettone and Vinyard, 1991; U.S. Fish and Wildlife Service, 1993). These findings led to the federal listing of both species under the Endangered Species Act in 1988 (U.S. Fish and Wildlife Service, 1993). Upper Klamath Lake probably contains the largest remaining populations of both species (National Research Council, 2004).

Life history and spawning characteristics of suckers in Upper Klamath Lake are understood reasonably well (Scoppettone and Vinyard, 1991; Moyle, 2002; Cooperman and Markle, 2003). Age estimates for Lost River suckers have exceeded 40 years, and most individuals reach maturity at 7–9 years. For shortnose suckers (SNS), ages greater than 30 years have been estimated, and most individuals reach maturity at 5–7 years (National Research Council, 2004). In both species, males typically reach maturity earlier than females. Both species are obligate lake dwellers and typically only leave Upper Klamath Lake to make spawning runs up lake tributaries (that is, Sprague and lower Williamson Rivers) between March and May of each year. Shortnose suckers spawn primarily in the Williamson and Sprague Rivers, but two distinct subpopulations of Lost River suckers have been identified in Upper Klamath Lake (National Research Council, 2004). One subpopulation migrates up the Williamson and Sprague Rivers, and the other spawns at several springwater upwelling areas along the eastern shoreline of the lake. Tagging data indicate a high degree of spawning site (that is, river or lakeshore) fidelity and little reproductive mixing between the two subpopulations (U.S. Geological Survey, unpub. data).

Although fishing mortality was eliminated with the closure of the recreational fishery, poor survival of adult suckers has been shown still to be a factor precluding recovery of Upper Klamath Lake populations (Janney and others, 2008). Upper Klamath Lake has progressed to a hypereutrophic state due to increased nutrient loading from wetland drainage, grazing, and timber harvest (Eilers and others, 2004). These conditions lead to massive blooms of the cyanobacterium, *Aphanizomenon flos-aquae*, between June and October of each year (Kann and Smith, 1999). The algal blooms and their subsequent die-offs produce water-quality conditions that are deleterious to fish health (that is, low concentrations of dissolved oxygen, elevated concentrations of ammonia, and high pH). Poor water-quality conditions are thought to have contributed to a number of substantial fish kills in the lake, most recently during the summers of 1986, 1995, and 1997 (National Research Council, 2004) and to a much lesser extent in the summer of 2003 (U.S. Geological Survey, unpub. data).

In this report, we summarize 2008 adult sucker run timing data and analyze capture–recapture data to evaluate demographic trends in adult LRS and SNS populations. Annual adult survival and recruitment parameters were modeled and compared to assess differences attributable to species, spawning subpopulation, sex, and year. In addition to estimating recruitment parameters from capture-recapture data, we assessed relative changes in length composition to provide additional insight into the relative frequency and magnitude of recruitment into the adult sucker populations. A comprehensive analysis of data collected up to 2007 is given in Janney and others (2008). This report is a continuation of the data analysis and interpretation reported in Janney and others (2008) with additional data collected during spring 2008 added to the analysis.

# Study Methods

## Sampling and Fish Handling

The Lost River sucker subpopulation that spawns along the eastern shoreline of Upper Klamath Lake was sampled at four known spawning areas (fig. 1) using 30-m trammel nets (1.8 m high; two 30-cm-mesh outer panels; one 3.8-cm-mesh inner panel; foam-core float line; lead-core bottom line) twice per week between February and May from 1999 to 2008. The only exception to this sampling schedule occurred in 2006, when each spawning area was sampled only once per week. Nets were set at each area starting at the shoreline and extended out in a semicircular fashion that encompassed the perimeter of identified spawning areas.

Lost River and shortnose suckers also were sampled three times per week from 2000 to 2008 during the same months stated above at the Chiloquin Dam fish ladder on the Sprague River. Before sampling at the fish ladder, a screen was placed over the bottom entrance (outflow) to prevent fish from exiting, and the upstream end (inflow) was blocked by a board to lower the water level in the fish ladder. A combination of dip nets and short trammel nets was then used to collect fish trapped in the ladder.

Additional trammel-net sampling for adult suckers was conducted from 1995 to 2008 at various sites in Upper Klamath Lake as well as in the lower Williamson River from 1995 to 2006 (Janney and others, 2006). A resistance board weir with a live trap (described in detail by Tobin [1994]) also was deployed on the Williamson River at river kilometer 10 from 2005 to 2008 to improve capture rates of suckers during spawning migrations (fig. 1). The weir functioned by restricting sucker passage to two weir sections. An upstream live trap was used to capture adult fish as they migrated upriver through the weir, and a downstream trap was used to allow downriver migrating suckers to pass the weir. High flows in the Williamson River during most of the 2006 spawning season inundated the weir and allowed suckers to pass over and around the weir without swimming through the trap.

Suckers captured at all sample locations were identified to species and gender and were scanned for the presence of a passive integrated transponder (PIT) tag. If a PIT tag was not detected, one was inserted into the abdominal musculature. From 1995 to 2004, suckers were tagged with 125-kHz, full-duplex (FDX) PIT tags; from 2005 to 2007, fish were tagged with 134.2 kHz, FDX tags. All fish were released immediately after being tagged.

3

## Remote Passive Integrated Tag Antenna Systems

In addition to traditional capture techniques (that is, trammel nets and fish ladders), detections from remote underwater PIT tag antennas were incorporated into the capture–recapture study design beginning in 2005; this was done in an attempt to improve the probability of recapturing previously tagged suckers. Suckers detected by these systems were not physically handled; however, those fish were confirmed to be alive and thus were counted as live recaptures in survival analyses. Locations of fixed, underwater PIT tag detection systems included: one each in the upstream and downstream traps of the Williamson River fish weir (2005–08); a river-wide array immediately upstream of the weir (2007–08); an array immediately downstream of the Chiloquin Dam (2008); the entrance, middle, and exit of the Chiloquin Dam fish ladder (2006–08); shoreline spawning areas (2005–08); and two river wide arrays installed in close proximity about 2.5 river kilometers upstream of Chiloquin Dam (2007–08; fig. 1).

## Survival Analysis

We used a Cormack–Jolly–Seber live-recapture model (Schwarz and Seber, 1999) in program MARK (White and Burnham, 1999) to obtain maximum likelihood estimates of apparent survival ($\phi_i$) and recapture probability $p_i$ for adult LRS and SNS. Apparent survival is the complement of the sum of mortality and permanent emigration (Pollock and others, 2007). Although temporary emigration may have occurred due to skipped spawning, radio-telemetry data indicate that permanent emigration out of Upper Klamath Lake and its tributaries by either species is uncommon (U.S. Geological Survey, unpub. data). Therefore, we believe our estimates of apparent survival were nearly equivalent to true survival. Lost River sucker data were analyzed separately on the basis of spawning subpopulations (that is, river versus lakeshore spawners). Lost River sucker capture events in Upper Klamath Lake nonspawning areas were excluded from analysis because the spawning stock membership of those fish could not be ascertained. Double-tagging data (U.S. Geological Survey, unpub. data) indicated that PIT tag loss in suckers was almost nonexistent and did not introduce substantial negative bias into estimates.

We assessed whether our data conformed to the assumptions of the Cormack–Jolly–Seber model using goodness-of-fit testing in the program UCARE (Choquet and others, 2005). Goodness-of-fit tests pooled over time indicated significant departures from frequencies expected under the Cormack–Jolly–Seber model for Lost River sucker subpopulations and for shortnose suckers. Lack of fit can be an indication of model assumption violations, sparse data, or lack of independence. Closer examination of our goodness-of-fit tests for individual time periods revealed no consistent or systematic bias that would suggest tagging effects. Lack of fit in our data probably was due to a combination of data sparsity at the beginning of the study, lack of independence, and spawning periodicity (that is, individuals not spawning in each year). The lack of independence (that is, overdispersion) probably results from schooling behavior and is relatively common in capture–recapture studies of schooling fish (Pollock and others, 2007). A quasi-likelihood correction factor ($\hat{c}$) was determined from the most general model for each species by use of the median $\hat{c}$ estimation method (Cooch and White, 2006; Lost River sucker lakeshore subpopulation $\hat{c}$ =1.44, Lost River sucker river subpopulation $\hat{c}$ =3.40, shortnose sucker $\hat{c}$ =2.26). These $\hat{c}$-values were applied to the set of considered models to compensate for overdispersion by inflating variance estimates. Applying a variance inflation factor is recommended when heterogeneity is detected, and supports a conservative approach to inference (Anderson and others, 1994).

A number of models were fitted in program MARK to the Lost River sucker lakeshore and river spawning subpopulations and the shortnose sucker datasets. The most general model in each set of models allowed for year and sex effects, and the year × sex interaction effect on $\phi$ and $p$. The most general model also incorporated a possible effect of PIT tag type (that is, 125 versus 134.2 kHz) on $p$ for the last 3 years of the study. We hypothesized that differences in recapture probabilities may have existed due to the greater detection distances of 134.2 kHz tags at remote underwater antennas.

Using the most general model as a starting point, models with fewer parameters were constructed by constraining $\phi$ and $p$ to remain constant across years, sexes, or both. Additive models also were used to reduce parameters (that is, achieve a more parsimonious model) and determine whether differences in $\phi$ and $p$ between the sexes were consistent over time (Pollock and others, 2007). These less-parameterized models were used to select a more parsimonious model and to test the effects of time and sex on $\phi$. We used Akaike's information criterion corrected for small-sample bias (AICc) and adjusted for overdispersion (that is, quasilikelihood AICc [QAICc]; Burnham and Anderson, 2002) as a statistical criterion to evaluate the competing models. Akaike weights ($w_i$) are reported to provide a measure of the relative weight or likelihood of each model being the best model in the set given the data (Burnham and Anderson, 2002).

Rather than making inference from parameter estimates using only the best model (that is, that with the smallest AICc value) in the set, parameter estimates were weighted based on $w_i$. Model-averaged parameter estimates account for model selection uncertainty in the estimated precision of the parameter and thus produce unconditional estimates of variance and standard error (Buckland and others, 1997). To potentially improve survival estimate precision and to evaluate the difference in survival between the two sucker species, we conducted a preliminary analysis using recapture data from both species grouped into one model set. We hypothesized that if differences in survival between the two species were small or at least consistent, then a more-parsimonious model with either no species effect or an additive species effect would be selected and would result in better estimate precision. Model selection results from this preliminary analysis, however, suggested a strong species effect and indicated that the pooling of data from the two species did not produce a more-parsimonious model.

## Recruitment Analysis

A primary concern in understanding and managing sucker populations is the estimation of changes in population size over time (Franklin, 2001). In addition to survival, recruitment can be estimated from open population capture-recapture data. Specifically, the reverse-time analogue of survival, termed 'seniority' and denoted $\gamma_i$ can be estimated. This parameter is defined as the probability that an animal present in the sampled population at period $i$ is an 'old' animal that also was present in period $i-1$. Population rate of change:

$$\left( \lambda_i = \frac{N_{i+1}}{N_i} \right)$$

then can be estimated without estimating either $N_i$ or $N_{i+1}$ using the formula:

$$\lambda_i = \frac{\phi_i}{\gamma_{i+1}} .$$

Pradel (1996) introduced a likelihood that models the entire capture history and is based on the temporal symmetry of capture-recapture data (Nichols and Hines, 2002). This approach combines probabilities describing forward time (that is, survival) and reverse-time (that is, seniority) processes, allowing the direct estimation and modeling of $\lambda$. The assumptions of the Pradel (1996) model are similar to those in the Cormack-Jolly-Seber model; however, the former also assumes that the study area is well defined and does not expand over time, and assumes no permanent trap response in capture probability.

The incorporation of underwater PIT tag antennas systems into our capture-recapture study design in 2005 created a situation in which previously marked fish have a much greater probability of being resighted than unmarked fish have of being captured, marked, and released. In essence, the underwater antenna systems create a dramatic "trap-happy" response regarding capture probability (Otis and others, 1978). This difference in capture probabilities does not create bias in survival estimates. Including remote detections in capture histories, however, would create substantial bias in seniority estimates and thus also bias estimates of population rate of change (Hines and Nichols, 2002). To avoid bias resulting from differences in capture probability, we modeled survival and seniority separately. Capture histories used to model survival included physical captures and remote detections, but seniority models included physical captures only. Early estimates of $\gamma$ are not reported because of poor precision due to sparse data and because it has been shown that the initial two $\gamma$ estimates are likely to be substantially more biased than subsequent estimates (Hines and Nichols, 2002).

## Length Frequency Analysis

Fork length (FL) of spawning LRS collected from the Williamson and Sprague Rivers from 2000 to 2008 and from lakeshore spawning LRS areas from 1999 to 2008 were used to visually assess changes in spawner size structure over time. Fork length data also were collected from SNS collected in Upper Klamath Lake and in the Williamson and Sprague Rivers from 2000 to 2008. Although this type of length analysis is qualitative, it was useful for documenting growth trends and corroborating evidence of recruitment, or the lack thereof, from seniority estimates. Length data were grouped annually by species, spawning subpopulation (for LRS), and sex to avoid size bias resulting from annual changes in species composition and sex ratio. We calculated recent annual growth rates for each sex of each species by tracking changes in the median of the dominant mode in the length frequencies. An average annual growth rate was calculated as the slope of a simple linear regression of the medians in successive years. The analysis was performed using the package mixdist (see Macdonald and Green, 1988) in the R software environment (R Development Core Team, 2007).

# Demographics and Spawning Characteristics

## Lost River Suckers

### 2008 Catch Summary and Run Timing

We captured 834 individual LRS in trammel nets at lakeshore spawning areas along the eastern shoreline of Upper Klamath Lake. Of these, 375 (45 percent) were tagged prior to 2008 (table 1). Systematic trammel net sampling at lakeshore spawning areas in 2008 indicated that LRS spawning activity began in mid March and continued through late May, and peak spawning activity occurred between mid and late April (fig. 2). The majority of lakeshore spawners were captured at Sucker Springs (35 percent), followed by Cinder Flat (26 percent), Silver Building Spring (23 percent), and Ouxy Spring (16 percent).

In addition to LRS physically captured in trammel nets, 5,801 individually tagged LRS were detected swimming over underwater PIT tag antennas at the lakeshore spawning areas. More individuals were detected at Sucker Springs than at any other shoreline spawning area (table 2; fig. 3). Lost River suckers were detected at the lakeshore spawning areas from the first week of March until the remote systems were removed during the first week of June 2008 (fig. 3). Only 12 percent of the LRS detected on the lakeshore remote stations also were captured physically during lakeshore trammel net surveys; 86 percent of the LRS physically captured also were detected on the underwater PIT tag antennas.

We captured 469 individual LRS in Upper Klamath Lake trammel net surveys conducted at pre-spawn staging areas in the vicinity of Modoc Point and Goose Bay between April 1 and May 2, 2008 (table 1). Of these, 62 (13 percent) were tagged prior to the 2008 sample season. Of the LRS captured at pre-spawn staging areas, 74 percent were subsequently captured or detected at the Williamson River weir and only 3 percent later were captured or detected at lakeshore spawning areas along the eastern side of Upper Klamath Lake.

A total of 1,319 LRS were captured in the upstream trap of the Williamson River fish weir. Of these, only 88 (6.5 percent) were tagged prior to 2008 (table 1). Most were captured between mid- to late April when water temperatures were between 10°C and 12°C (fig. 4). The remote PIT tag antennas at the weir (that is, the upstream and downstream trap antennas, and river-wide array) detected 7,920 individual LRS between February 20 and June 1, 2008. High streamflow during mid-April likely reduced the efficiency of the weir trap to capture suckers; however, the high flows coincided with a decrease in water temperature that may have delayed spawning runs (fig. 4). There also was a reduction in upstream trap antenna detections coinciding with the decrease in temperature and increased river flows (fig. 5).

We captured 507 individual LRS in the Chiloquin Dam fish ladder on the Sprague River in 2008 (table 1). Of these, 52 percent were tagged prior to 2008. Lost River suckers were first captured in the fish ladder on March 26 but peak catches and remote detections did not occur until late April when water temperatures were between 10°C and 15°C (fig. 6). The remote PIT tag antennas installed at the downstream entrance, the middle ladder cell, and the upstream exit of the fish ladder detected 883 individual LRS between March 11 and June 8. Most were detected on the antenna located at the downstream entrance of the fish ladder. The middle antenna detected 152 individual LRS, although the antenna at the upstream exit of the ladder detected only 11 individuals. Seventy-five percent of LRS detected at the entrance of the fish ladder in 2008 were tagged prior to 2008. In 2008, the additional river-wide antenna array installed about 75 m below Chiloquin Dam detected 2,700 individual LRS between March 15 and June 8, 2008. Of these, only 21 percent also were detected on the antenna at the entrance to the fish ladder.

## Survival and Recruitment Analysis

### Upper Klamath Lake Shoreline Spawning Subpopulation

Between February and May 1999–2008, we captured, tagged, and released 3,780 female and 5,728 male Lost River suckers at lakeshore spawning areas. Of these, we subsequently recaptured or remotely detected 2,794 females and 4,006 males on at least one occasion. Ten candidate Cormack-Jolly-Seber type models were fitted for the lakeshore Lost River sucker subpopulation (table 3). According to QAICc values, the best model had additive sex and year effects for $\phi$ and sex, year, and tag type effects for $p$. This model accounted for most of the $w_i$ (73 percent) assigned to the candidate models. Model-averaged estimates varied to some extent by year, and female survival was consistently, albeit only slightly, higher than male survival (fig. 8). Estimate precision improved substantially in later years when remote PIT tag antenna systems became incorporated into the study design. With the exception of 2002, survival probabilities for the shoreline spawning LRS subpopulation were within the range expected from a healthy population exhibiting a long-lived, late maturing life history strategy.

Because capture histories constructed for recruitment analysis consisted only of physical captures, seniority parameter sampling variances were substantially larger than those of survival estimates. On the basis of QAICc values, the best model had a sex effect but no year effect for $\gamma$ and additive sex and year effects for $p$. This model accounted for the majority of the $w_i$ (67 percent) assigned to the candidate models. Model-averaged estimates varied little by year and were consistently above 0.95 for both sexes, suggesting only minor recruitment of new spawning adults into the lakeshore spawning subpopulation between 2001 and 2007 (fig. 8). Estimates were consistently, albeit slightly, higher for male than females (that is, fewer male recruits). Seniority probability estimates were mostly higher than survival estimates suggesting consistent but only slightly declining LRS numbers for the lakeshore spawning subpopulation since 2001.

### Sprague and Williamson River Spawning Subpopulation

Between 2000 and 2008, we tagged and released 8,901 female Lost River suckers and 6,157 males in the Williamson and Sprague Rivers. Of these, we subsequently recaptured or remotely detected 5,530 females and 3,605 males on at least one occasion. The structure of the top ranked model for river spawning Lost River suckers was the same as the one described above for the lakeshore-spawning subpopulation, except the river spawning subpopulation also exhibited a strong tag-type effect (that is, 125 kHz vs. 134.2 kHz PIT tags) on survival. The model-averaged $\phi$ estimates varied by year, and female $\phi$ consistently but only slightly exceeded male $\phi$ ( fig. 9). Comparisons of $\phi$ estimate effect size and 95 percent CIs between the two subpopulations suggest that $\phi$ of the river spawning segment was substantially lower than that of the lakeshore segment in 2001. Modeling results indicated that survival in 2005 and 2006 was substantially lower for fish marked with 125 kHz tags (2000–04) than for fish marked with 134.2 kHz PIT tags (2005–06) (fig. 9). The tag type effect on survival was not an *A priori* hypothesis, but rather an exploratory *ad hoc* model that was run to determine if the overall fit of our most general model could be improved. We do not expect that this effect is a result of technical issues associated with the type of tag (e.g., higher failure or loss of 125 kHz tags) because models including this effect were not supported in analyses for either the LRS lakeshore spawning segment or the SNS population. Technical issues would be expected to show up in any population or spawning segment in which 125 kHz tags were used. We suspect that what shows up as an effect on survival due to the type of PIT tag is likely attributable to an interaction between changes in our sampling scheme and substructuring of the river-spawning LRS population. Groups of spawning LRS appear to be fidelic to certain sections of the river, with some fish migrating farther than others. Fish tagged recently with 134 kHz tags, particularly those that spawn lower in the river, have not had as many opportunities to be captured or detected. We expect that as more years of data are collected, this effect will become less pronounced.

## Length-Composition Analysis

Length frequencies of Lost River suckers captured in trammel net sampling at Upper Klamath Lake lakeshore spawning areas showed very little size diversity (fig. 10) and a steadily declining percentage of fish that could be considered recruitment size (Janney and others, 2008). These length frequencies corroborate with seniority probability estimates obtained from capture-recapture data that indicate very little recruitment of new adults into the lakeshore spawning LRS subpopulation. The dominant group or cohort of male lakeshore spawning LRS grew approximately 10 mm FL (fork length) per year between 1999 and 2008, and females grew approximately 12 mm/yr during the same period (fig. 11). Size frequencies of male and female LRS captured during spawning surveys in the Sprague and Williamson Rivers show a similar trend; however, the river subpopulation was on average slightly smaller and exhibited slightly slower growth rates (figs. 11 and 12). Both Upper Klamath Lake spawning subpopulations exhibited substantially slower growth rates than LRS in Clear Lake Reservoir, CA (Barry and others, 2009). The disparity in growth rates between the two systems is likely a result of a younger (that is, lower on the growth curve) LRS population in Clear Lake.

## Shortnose Suckers

## 2008 Catch Summary and Run Timing

We captured 672 SNS in trammel nets at Upper Klamath Lake pre-spawn staging areas in the vicinity of Modoc Point and Goose Bay. Of these, 137 (20 percent) had been tagged in a previous year. Eighty-five percent of the SNS captured in Upper Klamath Lake trammel net samples were later detected on antenna arrays in the Williamson and Sprague Rivers. Only five SNS were captured during trammel net sampling at lakeshore spawning areas. Underwater PIT tag antennas detected 42 individual SNS at lakeshore spawning areas with most detections occurring in mid- to late May. Only six individual SNS that were captured, tagged, and released at Upper Klamath Lake pre-spawn staging areas were subsequently detected at the lakeshore spawning areas during the 2008 field season. Four of the six were detected at the shoreline areas after being detected earlier in the sample season at the Williamson River fish weir.

We captured 288 SNS in the Williamson River weir trap, 68 (24 percent) of which were tagged prior to 2008. The three remote underwater PIT tag antenna systems at the weir detected a total of 4,061 individual SNS between February 20 and June 1, 2008 (table 2). The upstream trap antenna at the weir detected 772 SNS. A peak in detections on the upstream weir trap antenna occurred between early and mid-May when water temperatures reached 10°C (fig. 13). An additional 92 individual SNS were detected on the weir array after the weir was removed at the end of May. These fish were most likely moving back downstream to Upper Klamath Lake after spawning. We captured 239 individual SNS in the Chiloquin Dam fish ladder more than 35 sample occasions. Of these, 139 (58 percent) were already tagged. The three remote antennas at the fish ladder detected 771 individual SNS between February 27 and June 9, 2008 (table 2). The downstream ladder antenna detected 764, the middle antenna detected 287, and the upstream antenna detected only 98 individual SNS.

## Survival and Seniority

Between 1995 and 2008, we captured, tagged, and released 8,743 female shortnose suckers and 5,553 male shortnose suckers. Of these, we subsequently recaptured or remotely detected 4,054 females and 2,088 males on at least one occasion. A total of nine CJS type models were fitted for the adult shortnose sucker population (table 4). According to QAICc values, the best model had additive sex and year effects for φ and year and tag type effects and an additive sex effect for *p*. This model accounted for approximately 60 percent of the weight in the model set, while the remaining candidate models together accounted for 40 percent (table 4). The model averaged φ estimates varied considerably by year; female φ was slightly and consistently higher than male φ (fig. 14). Shortnose sucker survival was generally lower than that of Lost River suckers and was especially low in 2001 and 2004.

On the basis of QAICc values of seniority models, the best model had no sex effect and a year effect only for 2006 for γ and both sex and year effects for *p*. This model accounted for 50 percent of the $w_i$ assigned to the candidate models. Model-averaged γ estimates did not vary by year except for 2006, and were consistently above 0.95 for both sexes. This suggests that with exception of 2006, very little recruitment of new adult SNS occurred between 2001 and 2007 (fig. 14). Overall, seniority probability estimates were consistently higher than survival estimates, suggesting a substantial decline in adult SNS numbers since 2001.

## Length-Composition Analysis

Length frequencies of SNS captured in Upper Klamath Lake and the Williamson and Sprague River areas indicate little diversity in the size structure of the population (fig. 15). Very few suckers that could be considered recruitment size were captured between 1999 and 2008 (Janney and others, 2008). Although SNS seniority estimates and model results indicated substantial recruitment into the adult population in 2006, very few recruit size individuals were captured during that year. The dominant group or cohort of SNS suckers grew approximately 5 mm FL per year between 2000 and 2008 (fig. 16). These growth rates are substantially slower than those suggested from length frequency data collected at Clear Lake Reservoir, CA (Barry and others, 2009).

# Discussion

The overall fitness of sucker populations in Upper Klamath Lake should be of concern given the low observed survival in some years and the paucity of recent recruitment. During most years, estimates of survival probabilities were lower than seniority probabilities, indicating net losses in adult population abundances. The evidence for decline was more marked for shortnose suckers than for Lost River suckers.

Model selection results and the effect size of annual differences in survival suggest considerable interannual variation. Our data indicated that survival for both species, but especially SNS, was sometimes low in years without any observed fish kills. This suggests that high mortality can occur over a protracted period, resulting in poor annual survival, but will not necessarily be observed in association

10

with a fish kill. In contrast, water-quality conditions during summer 2003 were thought to be especially poor (Wood and others, 2005) and 53 adult Lost River suckers and 29 shortnose suckers were found dead during that summer (U.S. Geological Survey, unpub. data). Survival estimates for both sucker species in 2003, however, indicated that annual mortality was relatively low. This suggests that although small, local fish kills can occur, such kills do not necessarily translate to high annual mortality at the population level. Available data indicate that poor water-quality conditions resulting from massive algal blooms are present every summer (Wood and others, 2005), but we do not know why these conditions lead to increased mortality in some years but not other years.

Comparison of effect size and 95 percent CI between Lost River sucker subpopulations indicated that survival was markedly lower for the river spawners than for lakeshore spawners in 2001. This suggests that although the subpopulations reside together in Upper Klamath Lake for most of the year, their population dynamics and status are different. Possible reasons for differences in survival between the spawning subpopulations should be investigated in future analyses. If differential survival is observed in future years, it may have implications for overall species status determinations and recovery goals.

Populations of both species exhibited a transition from mostly old individuals, little size diversity, and consistently poor recruitment in the late 1980s and early 1990s to primarily small, recruit-sized fish and few large individuals by the late 1990s (Janney and others, 2008). This marked shift in size structure to smaller individuals suggests that substantial recruitment into sucker spawning populations occurred sometime during the 1990s. In recent years, populations of both species have exhibited a slow increase in median FL (5–12 mm/yr) and have exhibited little size diversity. This homogeneous size structure suggests that the populations contain mostly similarly aged individuals and that recent recruitment is almost nonexistent.

A common difficulty in capture–recapture studies is that parameter estimate precision and effective modeling depend not only on the number of individuals marked and released but also on the number that survive and are subsequently captured again (Williams and others, 2002). Due to the sparsity of recapture data, a number of the survival estimates from the beginning of this study had wide 95 percent CIs or were estimated on a boundary and therefore were of limited value. In addition to increases in sampling effort and consistency in 2000, remote underwater PIT tag detection systems were incorporated into the study design in 2005. The use of this relatively new technology improved recapture probabilities by an order of magnitude and dramatically improved the precision of survival estimates. These improvements will allow future analyses to begin investigating the roles that algal blooms, water quality, disease, and water management play in sucker population dynamics.

# Acknowledgments

The authors of this report would like to thank Mathew Abel, Nolan Banish, Ryan Braham, Nathan Harris, and Jody Pope for their hard work, dedication, and attention to detail. They were crucial to the success of this project. David R. Anderson provided invaluable advice concerning data analysis. We would also like to thank Scott Vanderkooi and Rip Shively of the USGS Klamath Falls field station for their assistance. The Bureau of Reclamation is to thank for the financial support and willingness to see this project through.

# References Cited

Anderson, D.R., Burnham, K.P., and White, G.C., 1994, AIC Model selection in overdispersed capture-recapture data: Ecology 75, p. 1780–1793.

Barry, P.M., Janney, E.C., Hewitt, D.A, Hayes, B.S., and Scott, A., 2009, Population dynamics of adult Lost River (*Deltistes luxatus*) and shortnose (*Chasmistes brevirostris*) suckers in Clear Lake Reservoir, CA: 2006–2008—Report for the Bureau of Reclamation, Klamath Area Office, Oregon. U.S. Geological Survey, Klamath Falls Field Station, Oregon, 30 p.

Buckland, S.T., Burnham, K.P., and Agustin, N.H., 1997, Model selection: an integral part of inference: Biometrics, v. 53, p. 603–618.

Burnham, K.P., and Anderson, D.R., 2002, Model selection and inference: a practical information theoretic approach: Springer-Verlag, New York.

Choquet, R., Reboulet, A.M., Lebreton, J.D., Gimenez, O., and Pradel, R., 2005, U-CARE 2.2 User's manual: CEFE, Montpellier, France.

Cooch, E., and White, G.C., 2006, Using MARK – A gentle introduction (5th ed.): Cornell University, New York.

Cooperman, M.S., and Markle, D.F., 2003, Rapid out-migration of Lost River and shortnose sucker larvae from in-river spawning beds to in-lake rearing grounds: Transactions of the American Fisheries Society, v. 132, no. 6, p. 1138–1153.

Eilers, J.M., Kann J., Cornett, J., Moser, K., and St. Amand, A., 2004, Paleolimnological evidence of change in a shallow, hypereutrophic lake-Upper Klamath Lake, Oregon: Hydrobiologia, v. 520, no. 1-3, p. 7-18.

Franklin, A.B., 2001, Exploring ecological relationships in survival and estimating rates of population change using program MARK, *in* Field, R., Warren, R.J., Okarma, H., and Sievert, P.R., eds., Wildlife, land, and people: priorities for the 21st century: Proceedings of the Second International Wildlife Management Congress, The Wildlife Society, Bethesda, Maryland. Hayes, B.S., p. 290-296.

Hines, J.E., and Nichols, J.D., 2002, Investigations of potential bias in the estimation of λ using Pradel's (1996) model for capture-recapture data: Journal of Applied Statistics, v. 29, p. 573-587.

Janney, E.C., Barry, P.M., Hayes, B.S., Shively, R.S., and Scott, A., 2006, Demographic analysis of adult Lost River suckers and shortnose suckers in Upper Klamath Lake and its tributaries: Oregon, Report for the Bureau of Reclamation, Klamath Area Office, Oregon, U.S. Geological Survey, Klamath Falls Field Station, Oregon, 42 p.

Janney, E.C., Shively, R.S., Hayes, B.S., Barry, P.M., and Perkins, D., 2008, Demographic analysis of Lost River sucker and shortnose sucker populations in Upper Klamath Lake, Oregon: Transactions of the American Fisheries Society 137, p. 1812-1825.

Kann, J., and Smith, V.H., 1999, Estimating the probability of exceeding elevated pH values critical to fish populations in a hypereutrophic lake: Canadian Journal of Fisheries and Aquatic Sciences, v. 56, p. 2262-2270.

Markle, D.F., and Cooperman, M., 2002, Relationship between Lost River and shortnose sucker biology and management of Upper Klamath Lake, *in* Braunworth, B., and Welch, T., eds.The 2001 water allocation decisions in the Klamath Basin: Oregon State University Extension Publication, Corvallis, OR.

Macdonald, P.D.M., and Green, P.E.J., 1988, User's guide to program MIX: an interactive program for fitting mixtures of distributions. Ichthus Data Systems, Ontario, Canada, accessed December 2008, at http://www.math.mcmaster.ca/peter/mix/mix.html.

Moyle, P.B., 2002, Inland fishes of California: University of California Press, Berkeley, 502 p.

National Research Council, 2004, Endangered and threatened fishes in the Klamath River basin, Washington, DC: National Academy Press.

Nichols, J.D., and Hines, J.E., 2002, Approaches for the direct estimation of $\lambda$ and demographic contributions to $\lambda$ using capture-recapture data, Statistical analysis of data from marked bird populations: Journal of Applied Statistics, v. 29, p. 539-568.

Otis, D.L., Burnham, K.P., White, G.C., and Anderson, D.R., 1978, Statistical inference from capture data on closed animal populations: Wildlife Monographs, no. 62.

Pollock, K.H., Yoshizaki, J., Fabrizio, M.C., and Schram, S.T., 2007, Factors affecting survival rates of a recovering lake trout population estimated by mark-recapture in Lake Superior, 1969-1996: Transactions of the American Fisheries Society 136, p. 185-194.

Pradel, R., 1996, Utilization of capture-mark-recapture for the study of recruitment and population growth rate: Biometrics, v. 52, p. 703–709.

R Development Core Team, 2007, R: a language and environment for statistical computing: R Foundation for Statistical Computing, Vienna, Austria.

Schwarz, C.J., and Seber, G.A.F., 1999, Estimating animal abundance: Review III, Statistical Science 14, p. 427–456.

Scoppettone, G.G., and Vinyard, G., 1991, Life history and management of four endangered lacustrine suckers, *in* Minckley, W.L., and Deacon, J.E., eds., Battle against extinction - Native fish management in the American West: The University of Arizona Press, Tucson, p. 359-377

Tobin, J.H., 1994, Construction and performance of a portable resistance board weir for counting migrating adult salmon in rivers. U.S. Fish and Wildlife Service, Kenai Fishery Resource Office, Alaska Fisheries Technical Report Number 22, Kenai, Alaska.

White, G.C., and Burnham, K.P., 1999, Program MARK: survival rate estimation from both live and dead encounters: Bird Study 46(Supplement):S120–S139.

Williams, B.K., Nichols, J.D., and Conroy, M.J., 2002, Analysis and Management of Animal Populations: modeling, estimation, and decision making. Academic Press, New York.

Wood, T.M., Hoilman, G.R., and Lindenberg, M.K., 2005, Water-quality conditions in upper Klamath Lake, Oregon, 2002–2004: U.S. Geological Survey Scientific Investigations Report 2006–5209.

U.S. Fish and Wildlife Service, 1993, Lost River (*Deltistes luxatus*) and shortnose (*Chasmistes brevirostris*) sucker recovery plan: Portland, Oregon, 108 p.

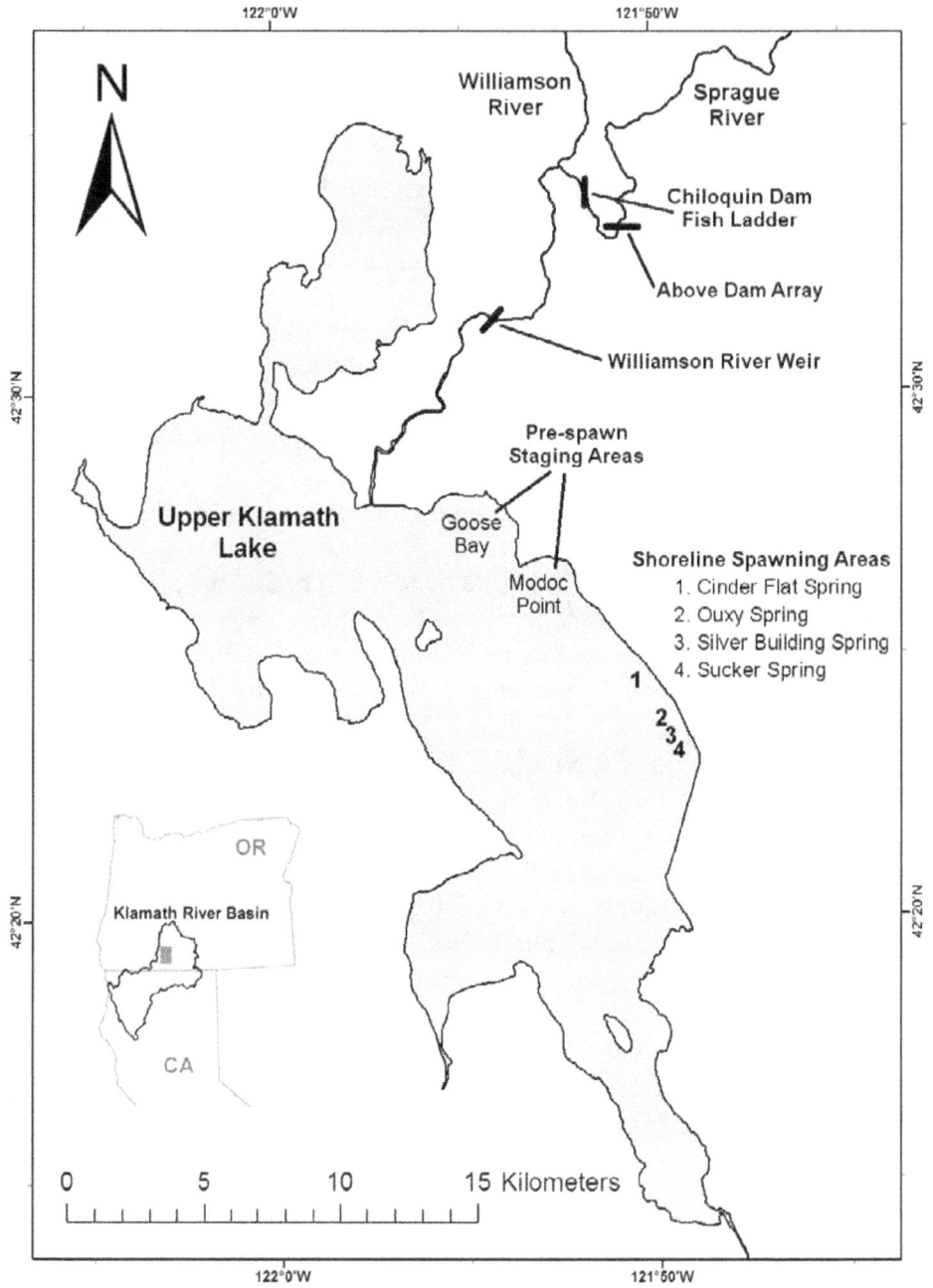

**Figure 1.** Upper Klamath Lake map, showing sampling locations for Lost River suckers and shortnose suckers. Inset illustrates the general location of Upper Klamath Lake in south-central Oregon.

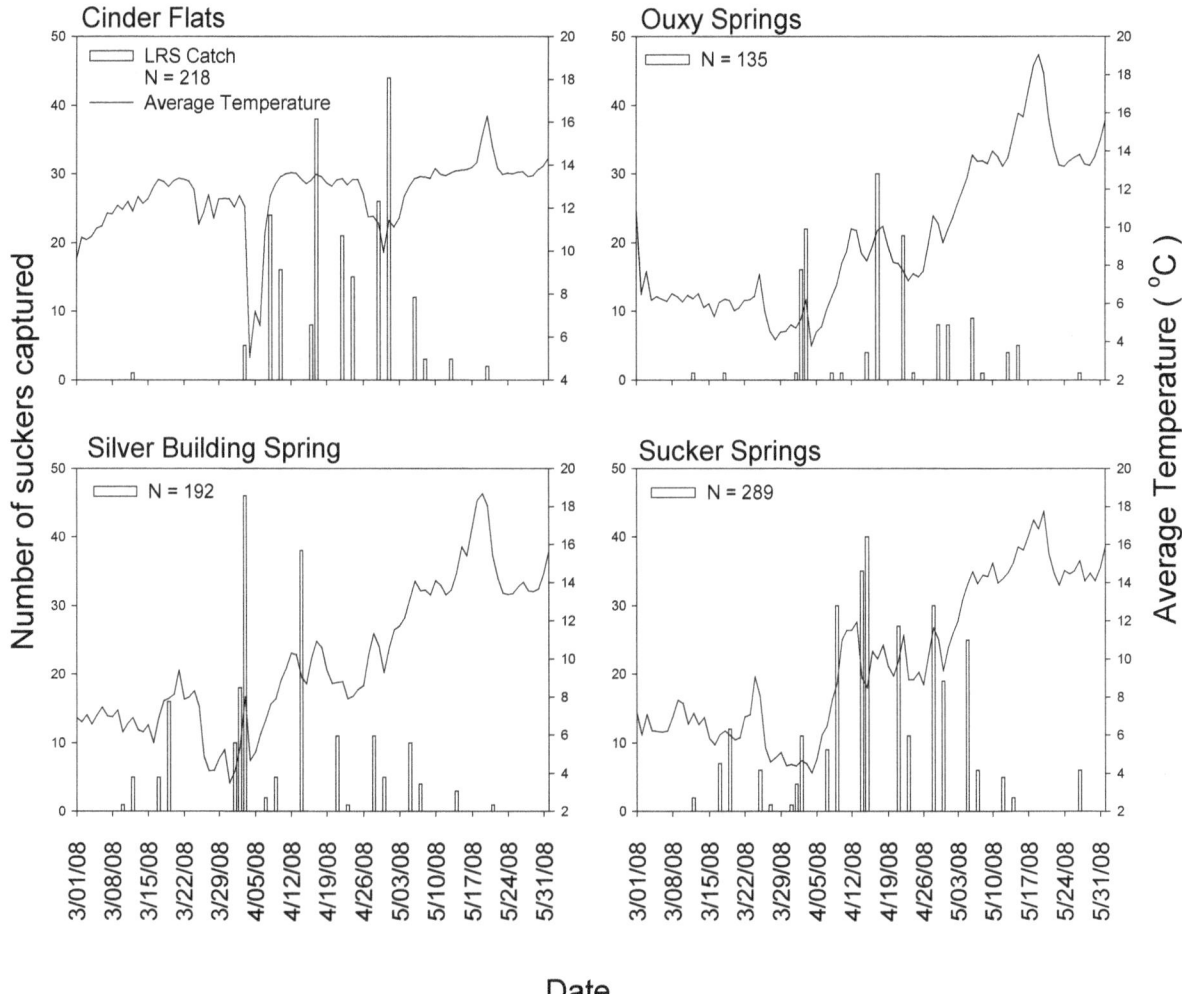

**Figure 2.** Number of Lost River suckers captured at four Upper Klamath Lake lakeshore spawning areas and average daily water temperature (ºC) in Upper Klamath Lake, Oregon, 2008. Temperature loggers were placed away from spring influence near each sample location. Only the first capture of an individual at a spring is included.

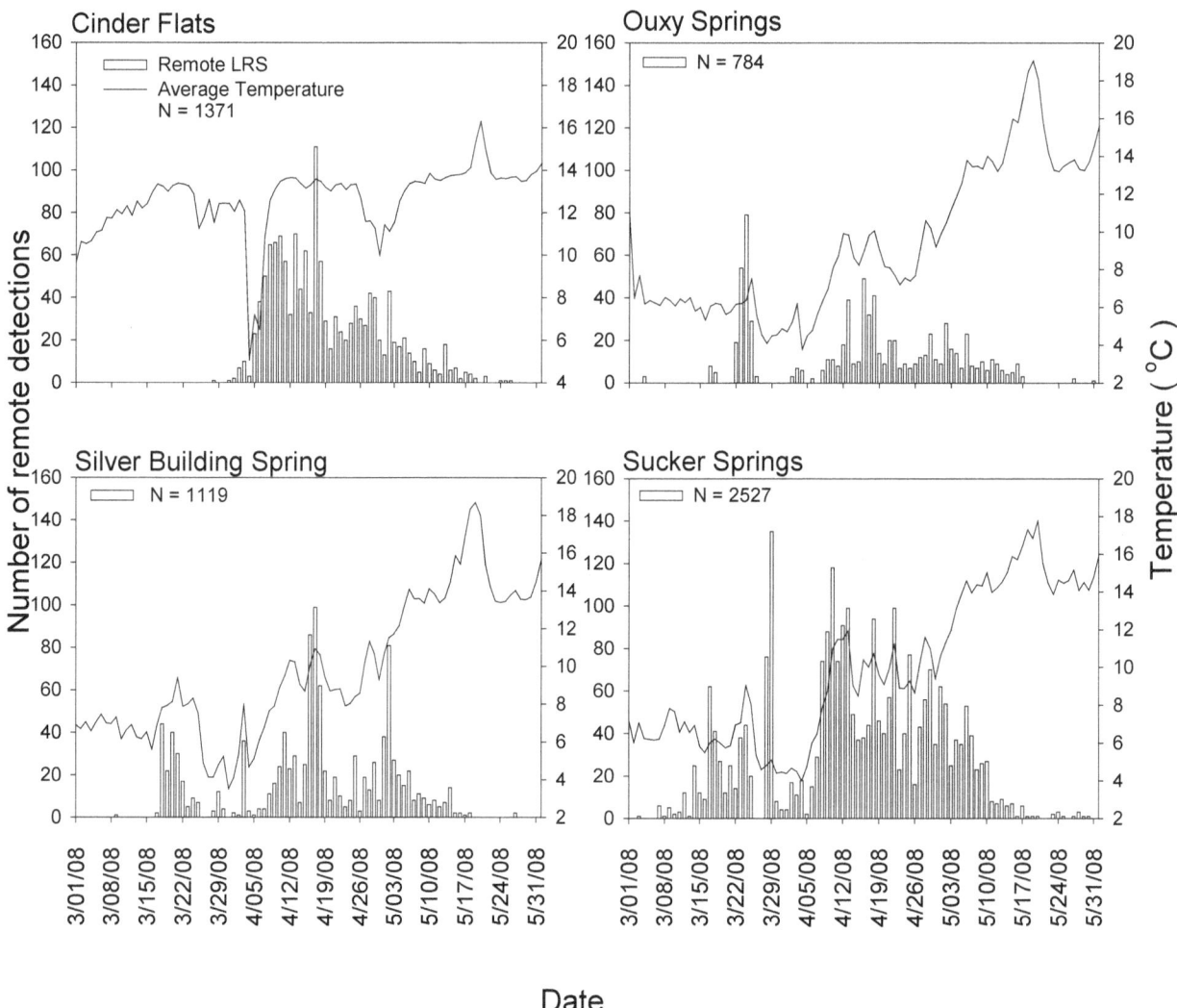

**Figure 3.** Number of individual Lost River suckers detected on underwater passive integrated transponder (PIT) tag antennas at four lakeshore spawning areas and water temperature (ºC) in Upper Klamath Lake, Oregon, 2008. Temperature loggers were placed away from spring influence near each sample location. Only the first detection of an individual at a spring is included.

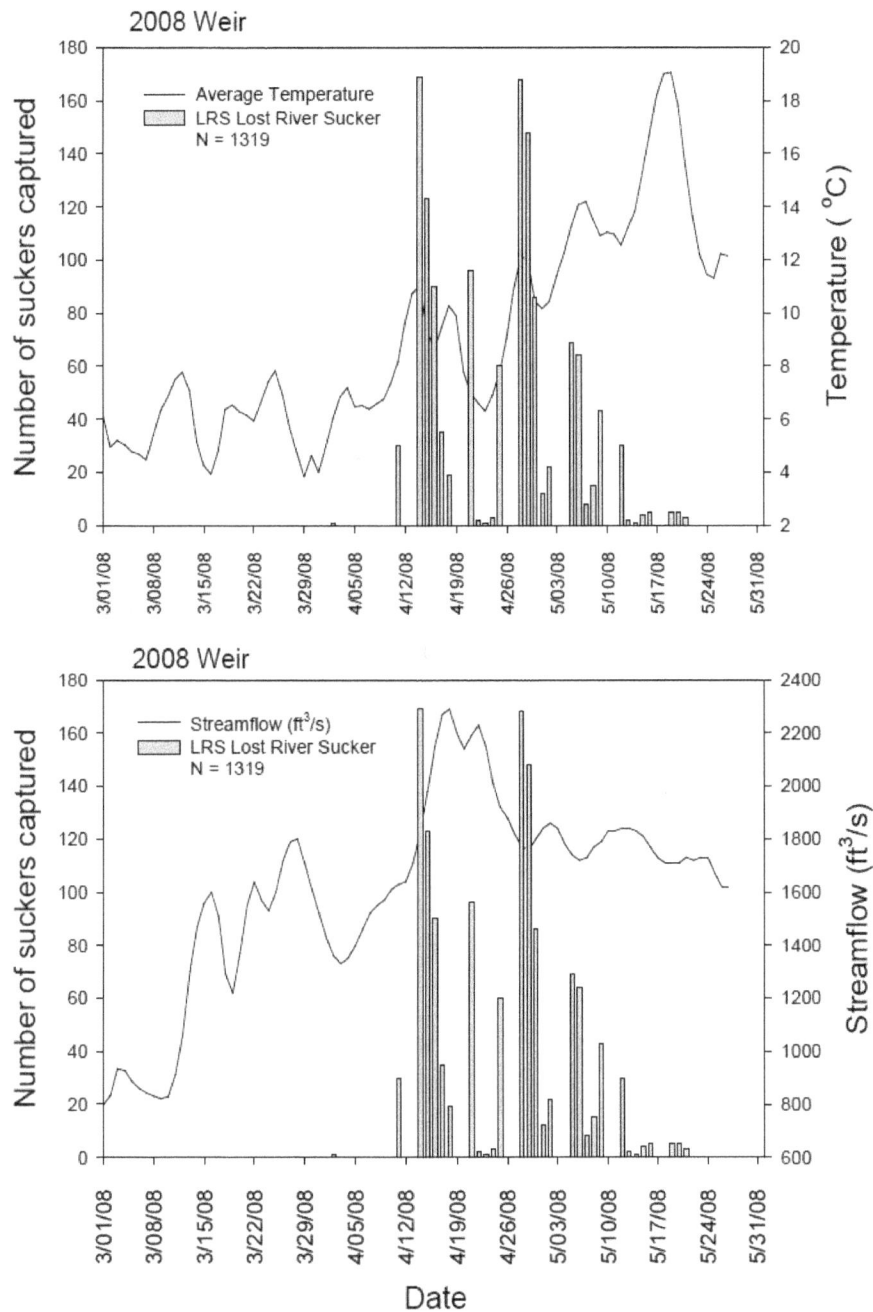

**Figure 4.** Number of Lost River suckers captured in the upstream weir trap on the Williamson River during the 2008 field season.

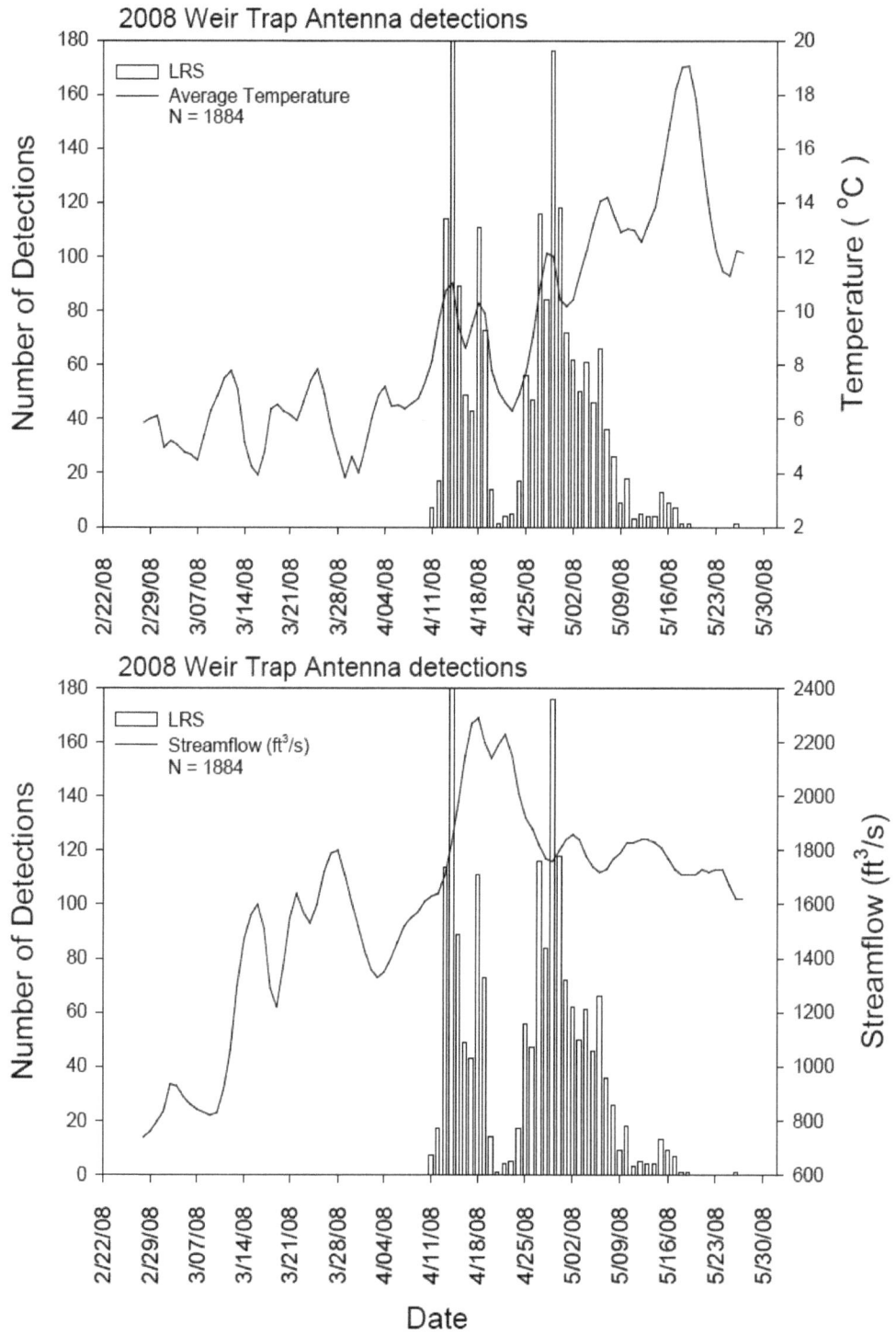

**Figure 5.** Number of Lost River suckers detectioned on passive integrated transponder (PIT) tag antenna located in the Williamson River weir upstream trap. Only the first detection was included for individuals detected multiple times on the antenna.

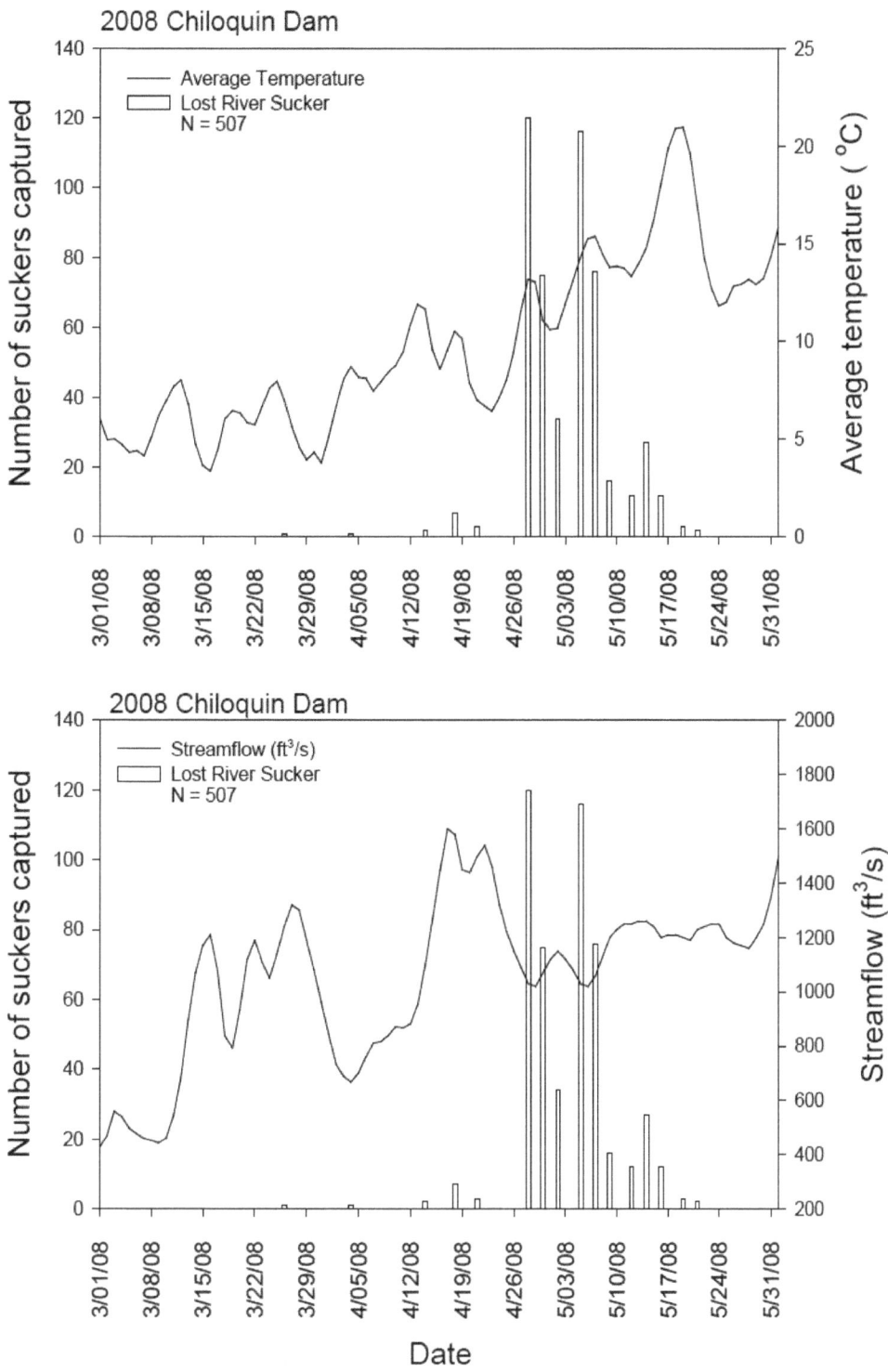

**Figure 6.** Summary of Lost River suckers captured in the Chiloquin Dam fish ladder on the Sprague River, Oregon, 2008.

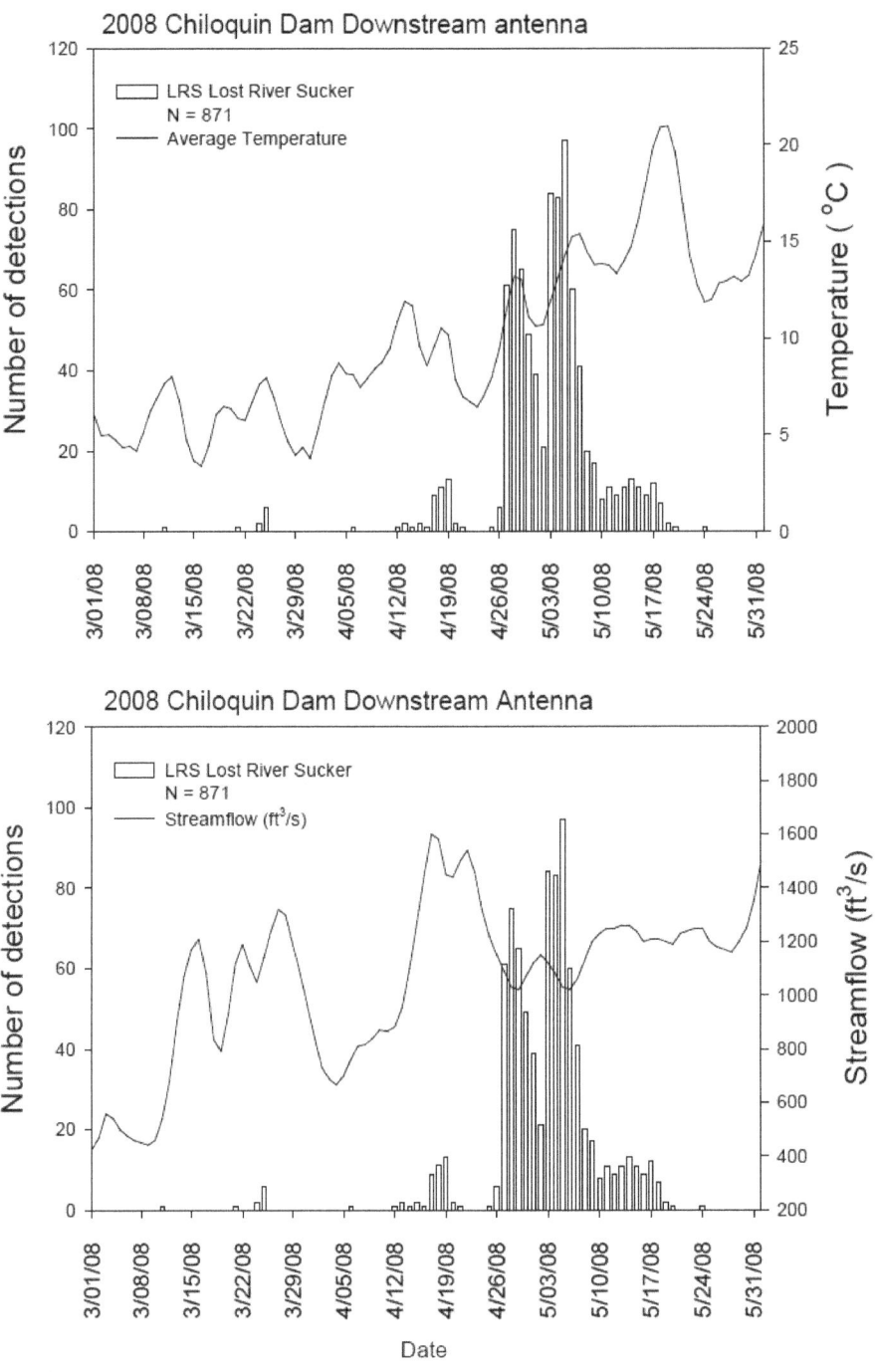

**Figure 7.** Summary of the first remote detection of individual Lost River suckers on the downstream antenna (that is, entrance) at the Chiloquin Dam fish ladder on the Sprague River, Oregon, 2008. Average daily water temperatures (°C) and stream flow (cfs) are also reported.

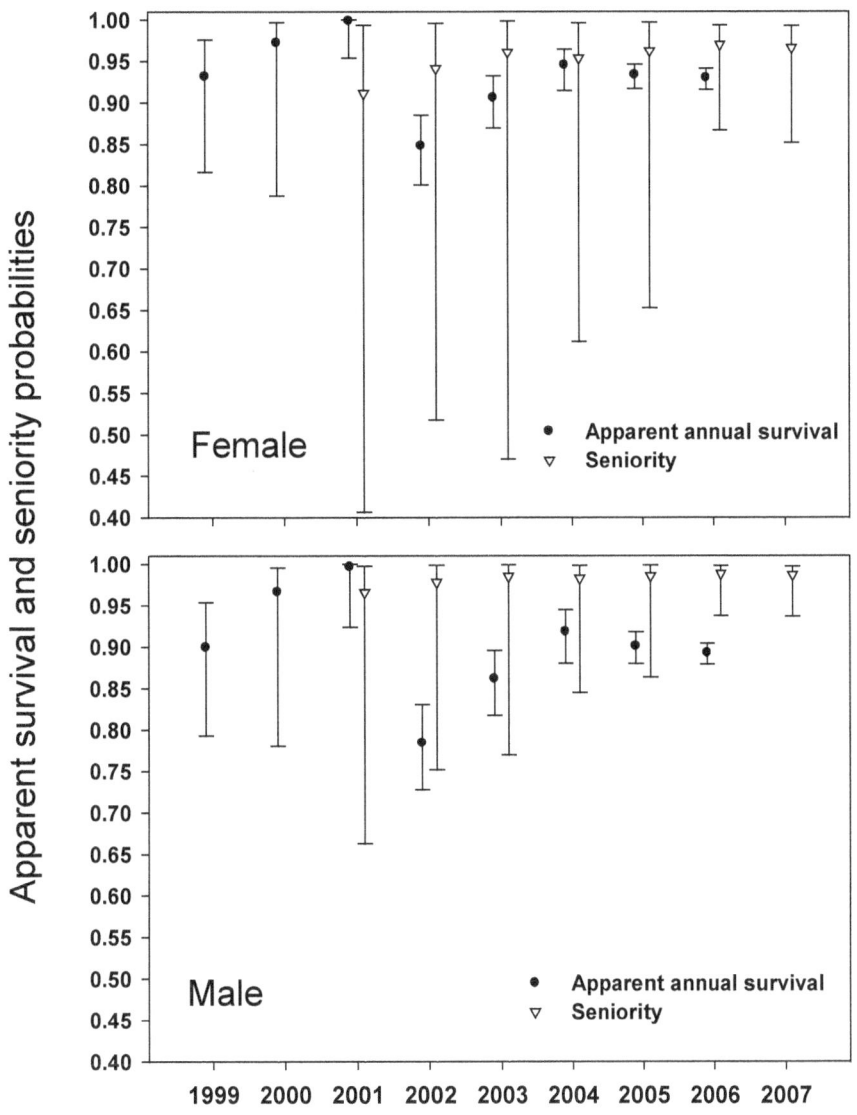

**Figure 8.** Apparent annual survival ($\phi$) and seniority ($\gamma$) probabilities (95% confidence intervals) of Lost River suckers from the lakeshore-spawning subpopulation in Upper Klamath Lake, Oregon, 1999–2007. Population rate of change can be estimated from $\phi$ and $\gamma$ estimates using the formula:

$$\lambda_{(i)} = \frac{\phi_{(i)}}{\gamma_{(i+1)}}.$$

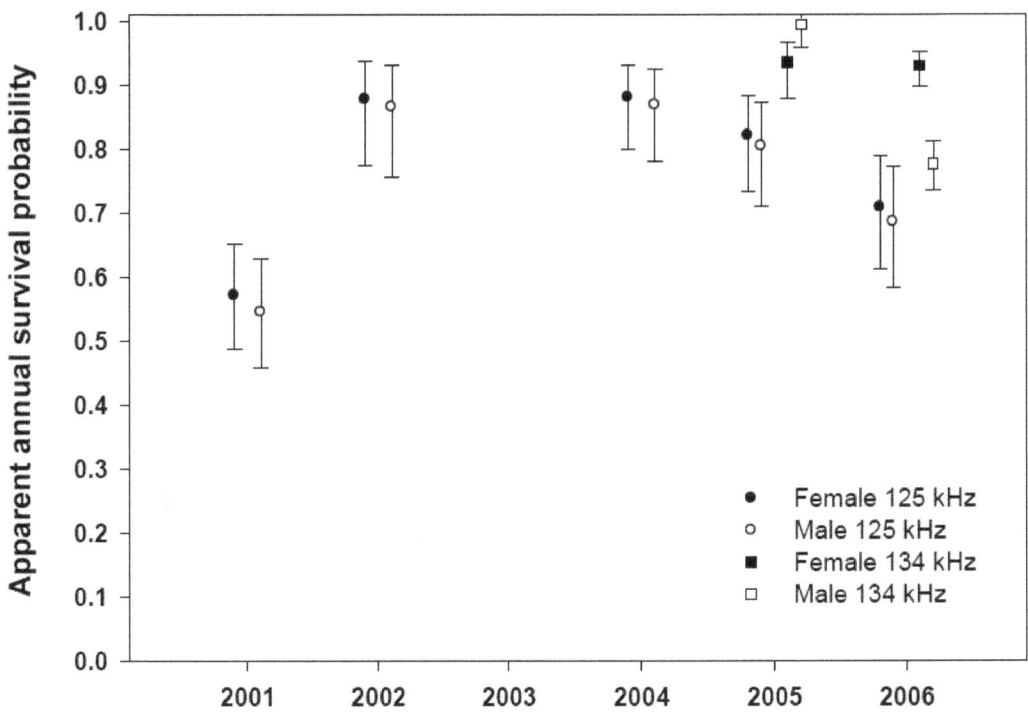

**Figure 9.** Apparent annual survival ($\phi$) probabilities (95% confidence intervals) of Lost River suckers tagged with 125 and 134 kHz PIT tags from the Williamson and Sprague Rivers spawning subpopulation, 2001–06. The 2003 estimates were on the boundary of 1.0, indicating estimability problems; thus, the estimates are not presented.

**Figure 10.** Length frequencies of male and female Lost River suckers captured in spring trammel net sampling at Upper Klamath Lake lakeshore spawning areas, 1999–2008. Dots along the x-axis represent median lengths.

**Figure 11.** Growth rates of male and female Lost River suckers captured in spring trammel net sampling at Upper Klamath Lake lakeshore spawning areas, 1999–2008, and in the Sprague and Lower Williamson Rivers, 2001–08. Growth rates were estimated by tracking changes in the median of the dominant mode in the length frequencies. An average annual growth rate was calculated as the slope of a simple linear regression of the medians in successive years.

**Figure 12.** Length frequencies of male and female Lost River suckers captured in spring sampling in the Williamson and Sprague Rivers, 2001–08. Dots along the x-axis represent median lengths.

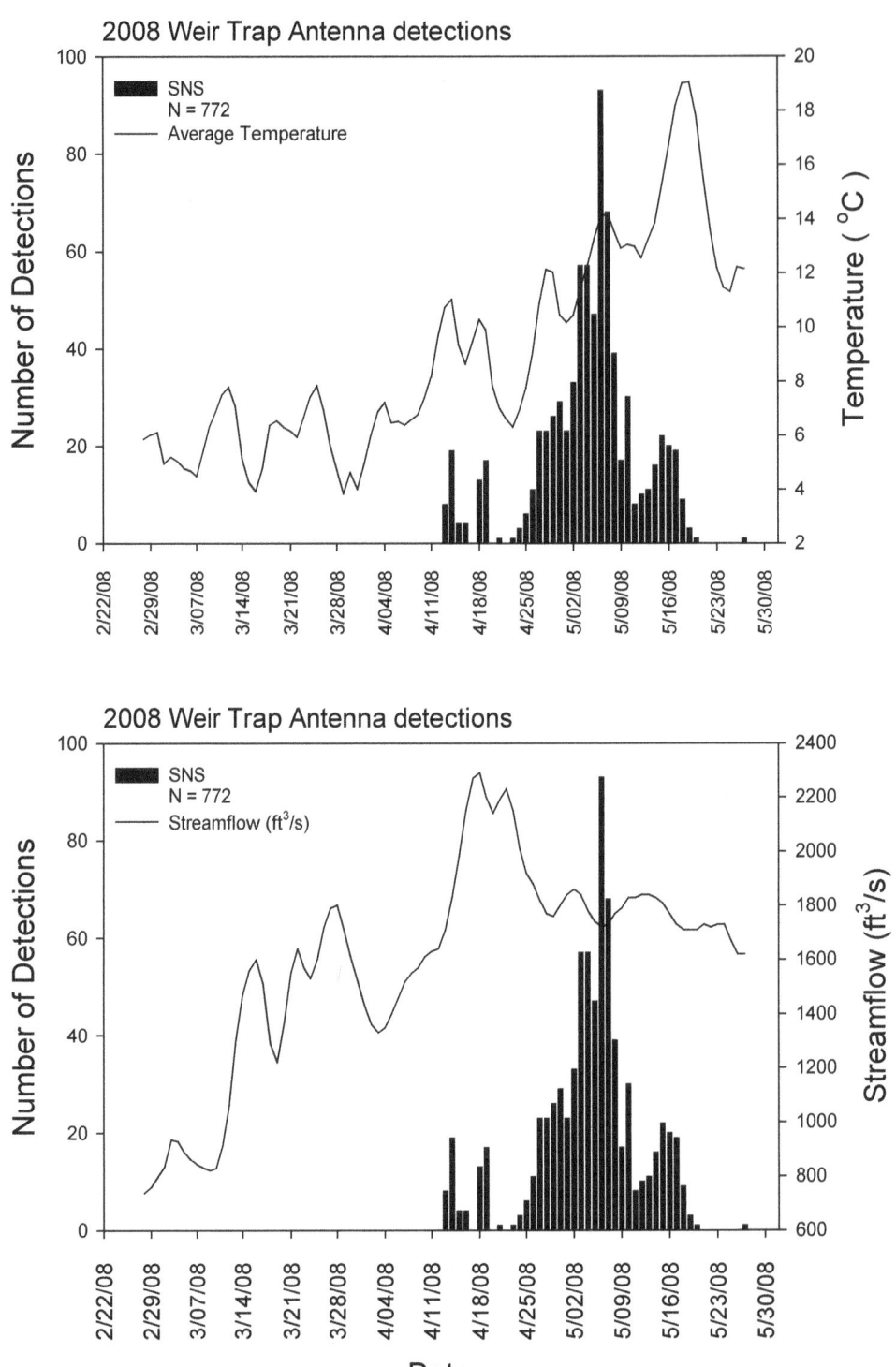

**Figure 13.** Summary of the number of shortnose sucker (SNS) detected on the upstream trap antenna on the Williamson River weir.

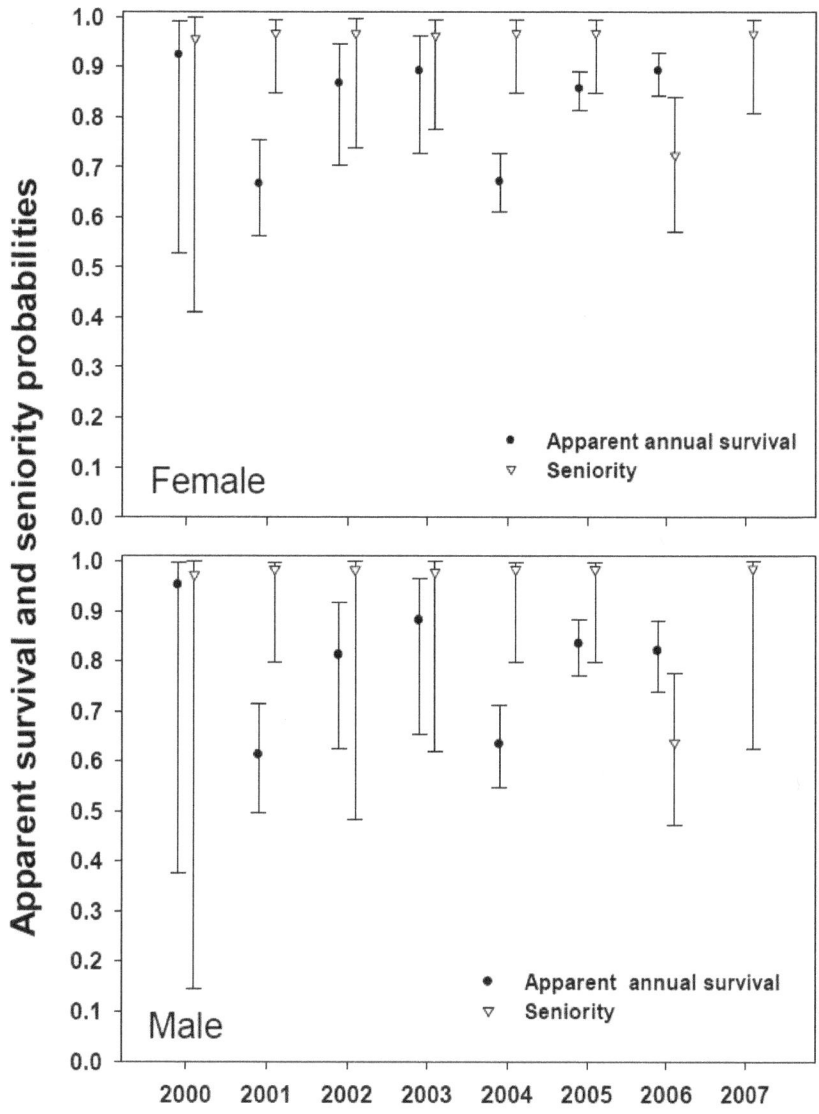

**Figure 14.** Apparent annual survival ($\phi$) and seniority ($\gamma$) probabilities (95% confidence intervals) of adult shortnose suckers in Upper Klamath Lake, Oregon, 1999–2007. Population rate of change can be estimated from $\phi$ and $\gamma$ estimates using the formula:

$$\lambda_{(i)} = \frac{\phi_{(i)}}{\gamma_{(i+1)}} .$$

**Figure 15.** Length frequencies of male and female shortnose suckers captured in the Williamson and Sprague Rivers, 2001–08. Dots along the x-axis represent median lengths.

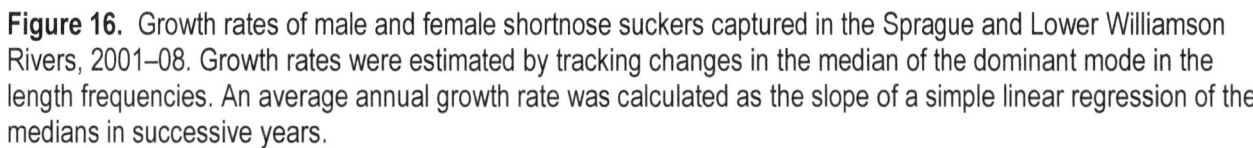

**Figure 16.** Growth rates of male and female shortnose suckers captured in the Sprague and Lower Williamson Rivers, 2001–08. Growth rates were estimated by tracking changes in the median of the dominant mode in the length frequencies. An average annual growth rate was calculated as the slope of a simple linear regression of the medians in successive years.

**Table 1.** The total number of Lost River and shortnose suckers captured in Upper Klamath Lake (UKL) and its tributary rivers in 2008.

[Totals only include the first capture at a location; however, individuals may have been captured at more than one location. Recaptures from previous years are the percentage of fish captured that already had a passive integrated transponder (PIT) tag]

| Capture location | Lost River suckers | % Recaptures | Shortnose suckers | % Recaptures |
|---|---|---|---|---|
| UKL pre-spawn staging areas | 469 | 13.0 % | 672 | 19.8 % |
| Williamson River fish weir | 1,319 | 6.5 % | 288 | 22.6 % |
| Chiloquin Dam fish ladder | 507 | 52.1 % | 239 | 57.3 % |
| UKL lakeshore spawning areas | 834 | 45.0 % | 5 | 100 % |

**Table 2.** The total number of unique Lost River suckers and shortnose suckers detected by remote stations in Upper Klamath Lake (UKL) and its tributary rivers in 2008.

[Totals include the first detection at a particular location; however, Individuals may have been detected at more than one location during the spawning season]

| Remote station location | Lost River suckers | Shortnose suckers | Total |
|---|---|---|---|
| *Williamson and Sprague Rivers* | | | |
| Williamson River fish weir | 7,923 | 4,061 | 11,984 |
| Chiloquin Dam fish ladder | 883 | 771 | 1,654 |
| Chiloquin Dam array | 2,700 | 777 | 3,477 |
| *UKL lakeshore spawning areas* | | | |
| Sucker Spring | 4,248 | 27 | 4,275 |
| Silver Building Spring | 3,492 | 17 | 3,509 |
| Ouxy Spring | 2,512 | 9 | 2,521 |
| Cinder Flat | 3,076 | 9 | 3,085 |

**Table 3.** Model selection results for ten candidate models of survival and recapture probability for lakeshore-spawning Lost River suckers in Upper Klamath Lake, Oregon, 1999–2000.

[Akaike's Information Criterion corrected for small sample size and overdispersion (quasilikelihood AICc [QAICc]; overdispersion factor $\hat{c} = 1.44$); values were used to select the best model from among ten candidate models of survival ($\phi$) and recapture probability $p$ for the lakeshore-spawning subpopulation of Lost River suckers in Upper Klamath Lake, Oregon, 1999 to 2008 (period symbol = parameter is constant over the given attribute; $\times$ = full model effects; $+$ = additive effects. The best model is presented first; $\Delta$QAICc represents the difference between the QAICc value of a model and that of the best model. Akaike weights ($w_i$) provide a measure of each model's relative weight or likelihood of being the best model in the set given the data. Number of parameters is the total number that is theoretically estimable by the model]

| Model | QAICc | ΔQAICc | $w_i$ | Number of parameters |
|---|---|---|---|---|
| $\phi\left(sex+year\right)p\left[125\,kHz\left(sex\times year\right)\times 134.2\,kHz\left(.\right)\right]$ | 22,778 | 0.0 | 0.730 | 30 |
| $\phi\left(sex+year\right)p\left[125\,kHz\left(sex\times year\right)\times 134.2\,kHz\left(sex\times year\right)\right]$ | 22,781 | 2.7 | 0.190 | 33 |
| $\phi\left(sex\times year\right)p\left[125\,kHz\left(sex\times year\right)\times 134.2\,kHz\left(sex\times year\right)\right]$ | 22,783 | 4.5 | 0.077 | 40 |
| $\phi\left(sex\times year\right)p\left[125\,kHz\left(sex+year\right)\times 134.2\,kHz\left(sex+year\right)\right]$ | 22,792 | 13.8 | 0.001 | 33 |
| $\phi\left(sex\times year\right)p\left[125\,kHz\left(sex+year\right)+134.2\,kHz\left(sex+year\right)\right]$ | 22,798 | 19.7 | 0.000 | 30 |
| $\phi\left(year\right)p\left[125\,kHz\left(sex\times year\right)\times 134.2\,kHz\left(.\right)\right]$ | 22,844 | 66.1 | 0.000 | 29 |
| $\phi\left(sex\times year\right)p\left(sex\times year\right)$ | 22,851 | 72.5 | 0.000 | 34 |
| $\phi\left(.\right)p\left[125\,kHz\left(sex\times year\right)\times 134.2\,kHz\left(.\right)\right]$ | 22,875 | 97.3 | 0.000 | 21 |
| $\phi\left(year\right)p\left(year\right)$ | 23,122 | 344.3 | 0.000 | 17 |
| $\phi\left(year\right)p\left(sex\times tag\,type\right)$ | 36,093 | 13,314.5 | 0.000 | 11 |

**Table 4.** Model selection results for nine candidate models of survival and recapture probability for the adult shortnose suckers in Upper Klamath Lake, Oregon, 2000–2008.

[Akaike's Information Criterion corrected for small sample size (AICc) and overdispersion (quasilikelihood AICc [QAICc]; overdispersion factor $\hat{c} = 2.26$); values were used to select the best model from among nine candidate models of survival ($\phi$) and recapture probability $p$ for adult shortnose suckers in Upper Klamath Lake, Oregon, 1995–2008 (period symbol = parameter is constant over the given attribute; × = full model effects; + = additive effects. The best model is presented first; ΔQAICc represents the difference between the QAICc value of a model and that of the best model. Akaike weights ($w_i$) provide a measure of each model's relative weight or likelihood of being the best model in the set given the data. Number of parameters is the total number that is theoretically estimable by the model]

| Model | QAICc Model | ΔQAICc | $w_i$ | Number of parameters |
|---|---|---|---|---|
| $\phi(sex + year)\, p(sex + year \times tag\ type)$ | 15,665 | 0.0 | 0.602 | 31 |
| $\phi(sex \times year)\, p(sex + year \times tag\ type)$ | 15,667 | 2.1 | 0.208 | 43 |
| $\phi(sex \times year)\, p(year \times tag\ type)$ | 15,667 | 2.3 | 0.190 | 41 |
| $\phi(sex + year)\, p(sex \times year \times tag\ type)$ | 15,682 | 17.2 | 0.000 | 45 |
| $\phi(sex \times year)\, p(sex \times year \times tag\ type)$ | 15,684 | 19.5 | 0.000 | 56 |
| $\phi(year)\, p(year \times tag\ type)$ | 15,695 | 30.2 | 0.000 | 28 |
| $\phi(sex + year)\, p(year \times tag\ type)$ | 15,719 | 53.8 | 0.000 | 29 |
| $\phi(sex)\, p(sex + year \times tag\ type)$ | 15,825 | 160.1 | 0.000 | 20 |
| $\phi(.)\, p(sex + year \times tag\ type)$ | 15,854 | 189.3 | 0.000 | 19 |

www.ingramcontent.com/pod-product-compliance
Lightning Source LLC
Chambersburg PA
CBHW080349290526
45791CB00009BA/2807